A Little Part of Me You Never Got To Know

Gina M. Poe

A Little Part of Me You Never Got To Know

Gina M. Poe

Copyright Year: 2007
Copyright Notice: by Gina M. Poe

Results in this copyright notice:

© 2007 by Gina M. Poe
All rights Reserved. No portion of this book may be reproduced in any form without permission.

ISBN 978-0-6151-5751-1

Dedicated to Wanda Williams
You always knew I would be something special and just look at me now!

In Loving Memory of My Father

Eugene Thomas Daniels Sr.

About The Author

I am a 33 year old female born and raised in Columbus, Ohio. Growing up, I always enjoyed writing. I never really thought that as I experienced different challenges in my life that I would find poetry as a way to express myself.

I have always considered myself to be a loving person. As I began to date and have different relationships, I could never understand how if you know what you want and your companion know what they want how someone always manages to get hurt.

As I moved on from one relationship to the next and things would bother me, I began to write my companion a letter expressing what I was feeling. Some of the letters they would receive and some they wouldn't. Some they would respond to and some they wouldn't.

I believe that after so many non responses you begin to ask yourself, "What am I suppose to do with all these emotions?" It can start to be really depressing. One day I was really feeling down and I felt I had so much to say to several different men I dated. That's when I wrote my first poem "Unsolved Mystery." I have been writing every since. Everyone needs to have a stress reliever. I thank God that he has allowed poetry to be my form of expression.

Gina M. Poe

Table of Contents

Part I **Confusion**

1. Unsolved Mystery
2. Separate Myself
3. Love Don't Make no Sense
4. Pain
5. Rejection
6. Still You Pick Her
7. I'm Crazy
8. What If?
9. Why
10. Too Late
11. Temptation
12. Addiction

Part II **Anger and Resentment**

13. I Can't Make It
14. Awww
15. The Ex Factor
16. Disgusted
17. Loving You
18. Love
19. Love of My Life
20. What about Me?
21. If Only I Could Cry
22. D Day
23. Why Am I Up?
24. I Don't Get It
25. Man Of Pride

Part III **Loving and Reevaluating**

26. A Healing Process
27. Heaven Sent
28. I Am Beautiful
29. Wisdom
30. Best Friend
31. I Owe It All To You
32. Son
33. A Better Place
34. Dear God
35. Loving Yourself
36. God, My Soul is Tired

Part I
Confusion

1

Unsolved Mystery

Inspired by the way you may end up feeling when you don't know if you've made the right decision in a relationship.

Unsolved Mystery

Alone again, yet **deep** in thought
Thinking of the **pain** men in my life have brought

More than *anything* it's plain to see
Men remain an unsolved mystery

How can you love me so much, yet speak so cruel
I'm infatuated by you, yet *I* look like a fool
You told me we would be married one day
I still thank God!
Good looking out!
I know that would have been a serious mistake
Without a doubt

More than *anything* it's plain to see
Men remain an unsolved Mystery

You came into my life when I needed a friend
Endless days and nights
Together
We would spend
I just knew this would be forever when you asked me to be your wife
How did it turn out to be the beginning of a lot of pain and strife?
We never made it to the alter
Just wasn't meant to be

More than *anything* it's plain to see
Men remain an unsolved mystery

Mm Mm Mm, putting my heart back together,
Telling myself,
Never again will **I** fall
That's when you meet someone **unique**
You know,
The greatest love of all!
Now this one requires patience
How do I explain it?
You want to prove to him you understand
Seeing *beyond* all his faults
Being **proud** to say
That's my man!
Once the initial attraction died down a little
I decided to open my eyes and see
This man I fell in love with was playing me
I guess deep down inside my heart
I couldn't say I didn't know
But I felt we had something **special** and I was determined to let it grow!
After so many lonely nights,
Crying myself to sleep,
I **had** to make a decision because **inside**, my body felt weak
After analyzing the situation
The bad outweighed the good
How can I get over this one?
I just didn't think I could!
After some serious soul searching and help from the man above
He introduced me to a new concept
I believe we call it **tough love**

More than *anything* it's plain to see
Men remain an unsolved mystery

Into my life you came
Nice complexion, physique, and hair
You seemed to be *everything* I ever wanted
So why was **I** so scared?
I felt I was always getting hurt, and convinced myself you would do the same
I tried to guard my feelings
Now I feel ashamed
I **know** in my heart you loved me
I wish equally, I could have loved you
You gave me something some women only dream of
That was a marriage and a beautiful son too
Why was I so quick to give everything up?
I only have myself to blame
When I think of where we *could* have been
I tend to cry and feel burdened with shame
Now that I've had time to think
What once blinded me
Now
I can see
It's **not** the *men* I can't figure out,
The unsolved mystery is me!

2
Separate Myself

Inspired by the way you feel when you're use to someone and you think it may be easier to try things again. The reality is that you just have to accept being alone for a change and move on.

Separate Myself

How do I separate myself from you knowing we've invested so much time?
I want to maintain a friendship
Is this *possible* without losing my mind?

I often question my feelings for you so I can come up with some type of solution
I ask myself,
Do I want you back?
I end up with this conclusion

I pretty much stay alone a lot, so you know I'm constantly thinking
Just to *hear* of you with someone else, makes me feel like drinking

What should I do?
We're suppose to be friends
Yet you volunteer *too* much information
It's been years now and I still can't take it!
However, there should be no offense taken

I need to resolve this issue
It's simply not healthy
They say you'll heal in time

But I must first separate myself from loving you
Relax, and ease my mind

3
Love Don't Make No Sense

Inspired by the way you may feel when you think you've finally found the perfect relationship and suddenly things change.

Love Don't Make No Sense

Have you ever met someone so *great*
I mean everything about them was *just* right!
You can be in a crowded room
And suddenly,
They're the only person in sight

Once you get to know one another
You've shared your dreams, wants, and needs
You start to get ahead of yourself
And you're thinking
I want to bear his seed!

Now this is where it starts getting confusing
Life never felt so great!
They say all the right things and you think…
This *has* to be my soul mate!

How is it that when you finally make it to this level
Things start to go into reverse
Everything you ever *dreamed* of wanting
Starts to fade
Kind of like disperse

What happened to the joy you shared?
You hardly even know them
All you wanted to do is prove yourself
Show them that you love them

They start pushing you away
You try to avoid the disconnection
They think of every excuse in the book
While showing no affection

Who *is* this person you thought you loved?
You will probably never know
They play you as if you should be *used* to this
Like you can just pick up your heart and go!

So here you are alone again with a thirst for love no one can quench
You keep saying to yourself time and time again,
Love Don't Make No Sense!

4
Pain

Inspired by the feeling you may get when you've had several failed relationships.

Pain

Please don't make me feel this again
Please, I'm just not ready!
This feeling I have deep down in my soul
Produced from something so petty

Why do I feel so naïve?
I don't seem to know the reason
God please help to ease my mind
And **except** that now, it's just not my season

I can barely breathe
Please don't let me go insane!
I can take this anymore,
I feel my life is going down the drain!

This is such a **sickening** feeling
Just make it go away
I just want to fall to sleep
Tomorrow, has to be a better day

Waking up I'm not surprised
I **still** don't feel much better
Where did we go wrong?
I have so much to say!
Would things make sense if I write you a letter?

I have to let go
But nothing was wrong!
The bloods racing through my veins
Thoughts of you fill my head
Adding stress to the brain

I often want to run away as I sit and listen to the rain
But what would that solve?
Absolutely nothing
So I pray…
God *please* remove the pain!

5
Rejection

Inspired by the way you feel when you still care for someone and you want to tell him or her but you're too afraid of what they might say.

22

Rejection

I want to call you so bad
Within the next five minutes, I **know** I'll have enough nerve
Pacing back and forth
Wondering what you're thinking
Trying to keep my heart on reserve
How would you react if I tried to show you some affection?
No, wait, what am I thinking!?
I'm too afraid of rejection

Are you just being stubborn?
Is that why we haven't talked?
If I only knew what you was thinking
I need to relax
Maybe I'll just take a walk
I can't ease my mind by drinking!

I *really* need to talk to you
It would be so much easier if you would just call!
Why am I sitting here wrecking my brain?
There's nothing easy about this at all!

Was there something that I could've done better?
Something I could've corrected?
I guess I'll never know the answer
I can't *stand* feeling rejected!

6
Still You Pick Her

Inspired by the way you feel when you're in a relationship and you find out there is someone else. Unfortunately, you're not the number one pick!

Still You Pick Her

I Love You, I Love You, I Love You
You tell me *everyday!*
I want so much to believe you
But the problems won't go away!

Stop saying things to me you know any woman would love to hear!
I thought that you were different
I mean, how will I know if the words you speak are sincere?

Please, don't say another word
Let's just go back to how things were
Because no matter how much you say you *love* me!
Still, you pick her!

You act like you accept the fact that this thing just won't work
You get upset and try to shut *me* down
But you look like the jerk!

Two weeks from now you'll be calling with another lame excuse
Like, I really miss you; I know I *love* you,
Well get over it!
It's just no use

You came to me with all these problems
And *plenty* of complications!
How can you have so much *love* for me,
Yet, you can't shake your current situation?

Please, don't say another word
Let's just go back to how things were
Because no matter how much you say you *love* me!
Still, you pick her!

7
I'm Crazy

Inspired by the way another tries to make you feel when they know they are the one to blame for the problems in the relationship

I'm Crazy

What *nerve* do you have coming into **my** life and playing **me** for a fool?
You made it seem like the feelings we shared **no one** could overrule!

You made me think you had matured
You knew *exactly* what you wanted to do
But as time progressed, you had tired game
I mean *nothing* you said was true!

All these things you say and do are getting kind of hazy,
Yet you have the *nerve* to look me in the face and tell me that *I'm Crazy*!?

You may not understand this part
It may be a little to deep
But when you tell someone you **love** them
It *should* be someone you want to keep!

You use the word so loosely
Do you even **know** what it's supposed to mean?
You made me feel like I owed **you** something
This feels like a bad dream!

See the effort you gave to be with me I found to be rather lazy,
Yet you have the *nerve* to look me in the face and tell me that *I'm Crazy*!?

8
What If?

Inspired by the feeling you get when you want to know how things could've been.
Later on you get the opportunity and all your questions are answered.

What If?

What if we really had the chance to be together?
Would you still want me as badly as you do now?

As I sit and reminisce on all the fun we had,
The way we used to vibe on each other's conversation
I can't understand why things turned out this way,
And I begin to be *filled* with frustration

You see time has a way of revealing itself
And a lot of time has past
Everything that made no sense at all,
Is oh so clear at last!

What if we had the chance to be together!?
Boy was that a joke!
You received the opportunity of a lifetime,
So how is it that you choked?

It's not that I don't feel like your intentions were good,
But I won't make up any excuses like maybe *I* misunderstood!
I heard everything you said to me because you see, I was thinking it too
So how did *I* end up with a broken heart trying to figure out what to do?

I could say a lot of nasty things simply because I'm hurt,
But I'll try the more mature approach by not putting your name in the dirt!

See sometimes we can get too caught up,
We tend to forget what's wrong from right
But when reality comes back to smack us in the face,
That's when we begin to fight!

What if we really had the chance to be together?
That's now a question of the past
I must do something more productive with my life
Time is just going to fast!

From what I hear you should never go back to a
relationship you've already had.
When I think of all the energy I wasted loving you,
I tend to make myself mad!

Goodbye my friend
I must move on, and this is what I know
This is a new year
There's no room for fear
So I'll start it by letting you go!

9
Why?

Inspired by the way you feel when things don't seem to be going the way you think they should go!

Why?

Why is it so hard to find companionship?
Is it that we're all just too afraid?
Or is it that we're just to caught up in our own selfish ways, trying to find the easiest way to get laid?

Why do I feel I have so much love to give, but no one to love me in return?
Am I that confused within myself?
How much more do I have to learn?

Why do I continue to make bad choices in men?
Am I attracted to the wrong type?
Or do I need to build the self-esteem within myself, so I won't be so quick to believe the hype?

Life can seem rather complicated at times and we tend to ask ourselves, *why?*
If we could just **stop** and think about the decisions we make,
That's when we begin to save ourselves from half the tears we cry

It's a shame how you have to go through things
It makes it hard to tell the truth from a lie
But if only we could put our faith in **God**,
We wouldn't have to ask the question, *why?*

10
Too Late

Inspired by the feeling you get when a person plays with your feelings time and time again. Then when they do decide to call it's too late.

Too Late

I'm finally were I need to be
As I wake I feel refreshed
Self-confidence is at an all time high
I can conquer any test!

I start by thanking God for blessing me to see another day
I then make sure my house is in order, and I'll be on my way

As I'm driving, my cell phone rings,
I wonder who this can be?
Hello I say with a smile on my face
Little did I know what was in store for me!

Why are you calling?
I thought we were done
But you thought you were *so* clever!
If you stayed away
I would calm down
That usually works, however…

This time it's different
Don't get me wrong
I'm sure that *you* are just great!
Sorry baby, I'm happy by *myself!*
So I guess you called too late

11
Temptation

Dedicated to those with cheating hearts

Temptation

Let's see how serious you are
I hear you talking to yourself
Convinced you are ready for a serious commitment
Can you resist me?
I'm with you all the time
Provoking you to do things that cause resentment

You and I was so close, living wild and free
I was the one pushing you, making you go get what you feel you needed
Now you want to leave me behind?
I don't think you are strong enough!
Did you forget…?
I was there all those times you begged and pleaded!

Suppose I don't want to let you go!
When you're not with them, I'll remind you of what used to be
I'll make you think of things you never thought you would remember, second guessing yourself,
Wondering, if you have the will power to live without me!

I can be your worst enemy when you feel weak; I want to make you become *filled* with frustration!
Who am I you ask?
I exist within you; I am none other than the *feeling* of
temptation

12
Addicted

Inspired by the way you want to feel every time you make love.

Addicted

Am I addicted to you because of your soft touch?
Oooh I can't believe someone could love me so much!
The things you say to me, the way you make me feel
This *has* to be true love; I know this time its real!

The way you hold me in your arms, *please* don't let me go!
I want this moment to last forever, I'll just die if you tell me no!
How did I get so lucky?
I've been blessed with the perfect mate
Someone to share my *soul* with
Wow, this feels so great!

Am I addicted to you because you love me?
I don't want to misunderstand
I mean the sexual tension between us has to be fulfilled upon demand
You touch me oh so gently, as our bodies are joined together
Your smile, your warmth, and the way you move
Nobody does it better
In the heat of passion as our hearts beat fast, and the sweat starts rolling down
Here comes the eruption, please no interruptions
As we harmonize in motion from this feeling we've found!

Oooh, now just hold me
Squeeze me close
It's just like we both predicted
As long as we keep making love like this,
We'll forever be **addicted**

Part II
Anger and Resentment

54

13

I Can't Make It

Inspired by that response you dread to hear when you were really looking forward to a date.

I Can't Make It

Can I see you tonight?
Sure, nine o'clock would be great
I'll have plenty of time to prepare for the date

Nails freshly polished, hair just right
Thoughts of you and me together,
Spending endless days and nights

I feel so excited
He should be here any time
It's amazing how things change
At the drop of a dime
Emotions overflowing
Excitement so high I can barely sit
The phone rings and I answer…
Sorry, I can't make it!

14
Awww

Inspired by the way you feel when you think you got played!

Awww

Awww, you got me!
Why do you do that sh--?
Is this some type of joke?

Playing with my emotions!
Standing me up!
I was your best friend when you were broke!

Awww, you got me!
I love you **still**
No matter how many times you call and don't show!

One day you'll look back and appreciate the woman *I* am,
Wondering, how did I miss out on Gina Poe!

15
The Ex factor

Do I really need to explain where I'm coming from?

The Ex Factor

You *must* be bored because once again, at my doorstep you've stopped
If I remember correctly, not once but twice
Am I not the one you continually decided to drop?

What's with all the games?
Do you know what you want?
If not, *please*, don't waste my time!
Everyone get's lonely, but give me a break
Our history resulted to you being a character in one of my rhymes!

Don't smile to big or poke your chest out to far
Listen closely, *this* I don't want to repeat
To even get close to me for a third time won't be easy
So tell me, can you stand the heat?

Technically, I shouldn't be wasting my time
You still don't know what you need to do?
Don't even worry about trying to impress me
Take time out to reevaluate you!

I'm looking for commitment
Try getting acquainted with the word
It's not a word that you should fear
I won't preach to long, just make sure you understand
I want to make myself perfectly clear

When you get weak and seek foreign pleasure, just because you are bored,
In Proverbs 18:22 it states;
"The man who finds a wife finds a treasure and receives favor from the Lord"

16
Disgusted

Inspired by the way you feel after a break up that you look back on and wonder what you were thinking.

Disgusted

I was patient all this time
And alone, I still remain
I feel I wasted so much time
Self confidence, I need to regain

It amazes me how I've become so turned off when I
attempt to even *think* of you!
You went from someone I fell in love with,
To someone I barely knew!

What were your intentions really?
Did playing with my emotions allow you to feel cool?
Not only did I love you once, I loved you twice
I feel like such a fool!

Only time could reveal how you really feel
In this case I believe you're busted!
However, my feelings were genuinely sincere,
Now, I remain disgusted!

17
Loving You

Inspired by the way you may feel when you know you love someone but circumstances just won't allow it to be possible.

Loving You

When I close my eyes and think of you, I try to imagine
how loving you could be
When I'm feeling sad, or I need a hug, you would be there
to comfort me

You almost seem to have all the qualities I feel my perfect
mate should have
The way we have a meaningful conversation,
And the way we make each other laugh

Just when I think you don't understand,
You call and you know what I'm thinking
We have a connection beyond explanation
So as I daydream, I try to refrain from blinking

How would it feel to welcome you as you come home
from a long day of work?
To massage you gently and allow you to vent as you tell
me about the argument you had with some jerk!

Just to hold you at night and go to sleep with the thought
that the love we share many are trying to find
To lie next to you with this feeling of comfort,
As my body naturally begins to unwind

Do I have to open my eyes?
Things are so perfect now, this is the one dream I want to
come true
However, reality sets in
And I've accepted the fact that from a distance,
Forever, will I be *loving* you!

18
Love

Inspired by my personal plea to the emotion of love and how I often feel looking for it.

Love

I just want to get to know you
It seems you're so hard to find
You are such a complex emotion
Thoughts of you are always on my mind

I often question if you really exist
Have we met and I missed the connection?
Or am I looking for all the wrong signs,
Leading myself in the wrong direction?

When I think of you I think of beauty,
Something innocent, and sincere
Just when I thought I found you
You always disappear!

If ever we should meet,
Please make sure I'm fully aware
Being blessed to share you with a companion seems to be
something I find to be rare

19
Love of My Life

This is the most emotional relationship of them all. The relationship that has you scared to try again.

80

Love of My Life

Oh my God!!!
What do I do?
I would've given *anything* for the opportunity to stay with you!
Where did things go wrong?
In the beginning or towards the end?
You were more than a man to **me!**
You became my best friend

What am I supposed to do now?
My every thought consists of you!
Never could I have ever been prepared for the day you would tell me you were through!

My heart is aching!
How do I move on?
Life won't be the same without you
I gave you everything I had!
Should I feel sad?
Should I feel mad?
Should I play things off and be cool?

Just the thought of another guy being in my life really makes me sick!
Wondering if they're real or if they got game
Hoping you make the right pick

Please let this be a nightmare!
I couldn't have possibly failed again!
Just when it's time to enjoy what we've shared,
Our relationship has to come to an end?

Right back at square one at the age of thirty two
I thought we would be together forever!
Now, I have a different view

Your passion was *powerful*
That's how I fell in love!
Our connection was greater,
Heaven sent, from God above

I know I'm not trippin
I'll never love *anyone* the way I've loved you!
I wish God would've put it in your heart to feel how much!
At least I would have the satisfaction of knowing you knew!

I never meant to break your heart,
That's something I wouldn't do
But I did it anyway without intent, and there's no way to make it up to you!

I really believe ending this was a mistake
I have too much love for you and a heart that's continuing to break!

I feel so pathetic!
I need to play this sh-- off!
At least that's what your homies would say
But I'll slowly move forward, with the help of god, to face another day

I loved you enough to work past any of your faults
But in the end I guess we were both two stubborn adults!

Well I love you baby
A special place in my heart, you will *always* remain!
I'll focus on the happy times to cover up the pain

Looking into my future, and not seeing you there, cuts just like a knife
But one thing that I can say for sure
You will *always* be **The Love of My Life**!

20
What about Me?

Inspired by the way you feel when the person you are in a relationship with seems to only think of their feelings.

What about Me

I was the person I told you I would be!
Now **you** are finished?
What about me!?

I thought we had something special that *everyone* could see!
Now **you** are finished?
What about me!?

My love for you was free and came without a fee!
Now **you** are finished?
What about me!?

I took the *I* away from myself and turned it into we!
Now **you** are finished?
What about me!?

When it came to *my* heart, I handed *you* the key!
Now **you** are finished?
What about me!?

What about me!?

What about me!?

21
If only I could Cry

Inspired by that feeling you get when you just need to cry but can't.

If only I could Cry

What am I supposed to do?
I feel so numb inside
Heartache after heartache
Little room left for pride
Trying to take deep breaths
Hoping to release frustration with a sigh
Life would be much easier
If only I could cry

22
D Day

Inspired by the fact that you know you have a decision to make.

D Day

I need to make some decisions, and I don't know what to do!
I can't seem to entertain the thought of not having you to talk to!

I consider you my dear friend because we have a spiritual connection
We can laugh, joke, talk, and play
Share just the right amount of affection!

So what am I suppose to do when I have such a hard decision to make?
My mind is filled with a million thoughts,
I don't know how much more I can take!

Do I let go of the type of friendship many long to find?
Or should I travel down this uncertain road,
And leave my fears behind.

23
Why am I Up?

Inspired by those nights when you just can't sleep and you wake up thinking of them!

Why am I Up?

Why am I up thinking about you?

In *your* heart,
Do I even exist?

My stomach hurt,
I'm all sad and sh--!

When you think of those *you* love,
Am I on the list?

I *really* feel rotten inside,
Like I'm dying from a body of rejection!

Do you even *care* that this is how **you** made me feel because **you** chose to show a lack of affection!?

Why do I feel like I love you still?
You chose to continue your life without me!

Do you love someone else?
Does she make you happy?
If yes,
Who could it possibly be?

So many questions,
Such little answers,
And I wonder why I can't sleep!

I love you!
I love you!
I love you!
I love you!

Man, I'm in way to deep!

24
I Don't get It!

Inspired by that feeling of confusion you get when you are in a relationship.

I Don't get It!

Didn't you say you were straight on me?
So why is it that now that I do my own thing you want to trip?

Stop acting like you were truly a friend to me!
Come get your sh-- and dip!

Why keep in contact?
What's the point?
Is there something you are trying to prove?

You build me up, just to break me down
So get to steppin!
I'm now dancing to a new groove!

I'm a little upset!
The man you said you were has *yet* to be proven!
Straight ahead, forward march, stay out of my life!
Keep it movin!

25
Man of Pride

Inspired by that special someone who can never admit to their own faults but can always find someone else to blame.

Man of Pride

Why can't you take the blame for the things *you* do?
When I tell you *my* feelings are hurt, the argument always
ends up about **you!**

Maybe if you would just listen to what **I** am saying,
You'd *understand* why the trust is faulted, and I found out
you were out playing!

All you had to do was give me the time *I* felt I deserved!
But you want to be upset that I was snooping?
Man, you have a lot of nerve!

It's *crazy* how you can allow yourself to close your eyes to
what you don't want to see!
So what *I* finally took the time to realize was, the friend I
chose to be to you,
You would *never* be to me!

You are to busy *worrying* about how things affected **you**!
But *you* chose to be in a relationship with **me**!
Try considering my feelings too!

Why do you have to have so much pride?
You have no *idea* how much I really love you!
It's like you get a *joy* from reminding me that we're not
together, and telling me how we are through!

You left me *filled* with emotion overflowing!
Crying in private day after day, keeping you from knowing!

But in your mind it's me you blame!?
Why?
Is it because I allowed myself to love you *so* much?
Wow, that's such a shame!

I hate to give up on what I *know* we could have had
But what's in your **heart**, from the outside, won't show!
So how much you really cared for **me,** is something I will *never* know

How much longer will you *remain* this way?
How much longer will the *real* you hide?
I **can't** continue to save *myself*, for a man that has too much pride!

Part III

Loving and Reevaluating

26
A Healing Process

Inspired by the fact that it is not healthy to start a new relationship if you are not completely over the one you were in.

.

A Healing Process

No one wants to be alone
So instead, what do we do?
We'll jump into another relationship
Not understanding, the only one that's going to be screwed is you!

You're scared, hurt, and feeling rejected
You're unable to show real love because your heart is infected

Your body is polluted by pain
You feel you have nothing to lose and nothing to gain

You're blinded by the problems of the past
Therefore you're unable to see why your relationships don't last

You can have someone that's faithful and true
Their main concern is to be down for you!

But you're still dealing with emotions from the one you loved and cared for
Paying no attention to the one you are with, so they feel rejected and find themselves begging for more!

You don't know what the problem is
But you know it had nothing to do with you
What you failed to realize is for a relationship to prosper,
It takes the effort of two!

You have to stop!
Take time out
In life you will be given many tests

But you will always fail
If you don't wake up and realize
That with recovery, there has to be a healing process

27
Heaven Sent

Inspired by the way you feel at the beginning of those relationships when you know you've found the right one.

Heaven Sent

Talking to you for the first time
Yet, I feel like we've previously met
The feeling of **comfort** just to hear your voice, Is
something you rarely get

Who would've thought we would be connected when you live so far away!
Just the **projection** of what *could* be, tends to brighten my day**!**

When two people meet, and the common denominator is **love,**
Know when to grab hold of your blessing, because heaven must have sent them from above!

28
I am Beautiful

Dedicated to those who need a self esteem boost.

I am Beautiful

I am such a kind and loving person
If people would take the time to get to know me, they would see

It's **not** the outward appearance that's important,
My beauty *shines* from within me!

Did I ask for your opinion?
When it comes to *my* destiny, it is ***I*** who holds the key!
I am the *only* one in control of what it is ***I*** want to be!

So the next time you try to greet me, but you don't have anything *nice* to say,
Kindly continue to keep walking, because I **refuse** to let you ruin my day!

For the longest time I was so caught up in what **others** thought I should be
But as I mature, I know that **I am beautiful**, and God has **great** things in store for me!

29
Wisdom

Wisdom

Positive, strong, proud, and **free**
These are just a few words that describe the ***real*** me!
Never looking back and focusing on **what** or **how** life *could* be
But **boldly** stepping into the future, ***unafraid*** of what I am unable to see!

30
Best Friend

If you are blessed to have one, keep them close because they are hard to find!

Best Friend

Thank you for listening
Over and *over* again!
You manage to be there constantly,
Qualities of a best friend

If I didn't have you to whine to,
Only **God** knows where I'd be!
Never expressing criticism
Just trying to understand **me**

True friends are hard to come by
I only have a selected few
Through blood I have a brother,
But a **sister** I've found in you!

You've seen me at some of my *lowest* points,
When all I could do was cry
You managed to turn it into laughter, giving advice like give love another try!

So as you travel life's journeys with me,
Stay prayerful that the right thing is what I'll do
I need you to stay **strong** for me!
And I'll return the favor to you!

31
I Owe It All to You

Inspired by the relationship between my mother and I.
Dedicated to Wanda Williams

I Owe It All to You

As long as I can remember, you've *always* been there for me
Fulfilling all my wants and needs
Pushing me to be all I can be

The closeness that we share has to be a gift from God above,
Because nothing could compare to a mother and daughters love

I'm so glad God gave me to you
I couldn't *imagine* a mother greater
I want everything I do to be pleasing too; I never want to regret it later

Did you know that spiritually you are my inspiration?
You make me want to grow
I love you mom and that's a fact
My feelings I'm not afraid to show

You always try to make life easy for me, time and time again
If ever I'm sad you try to lift me up
You *truly* are my best friend

How can I ever repay you?
It seems like you are always helping me
One day I'll be blessed
God will handle the rest
And I'll let you live debt free!

So sit back and relax
As I continue to grow
Because there's something you always knew
When I finally prosper in what God has me to do
I can say, I owe it *all* to you!

32
Son

Inspired by the relationship I have with my son and the questions you sometimes have as a single parent. Dedicated to Andre J. Poe Jr.

Son

Am I doing this whole mothering thing right?
I know you're too small to answer
Raising you alone gets hard at times
But this is what I want you to remember

I want the best for you so I work real hard
I want to provide you with the things you need
I promise to be there every step of the way
Making sure that you succeed

I know I'm not the funniest mommy
I can't let you do everything that you want to do
See as you get older then you'll understand, my first priority is you

I want you to always feel close to me
I love you with all my heart,
Hopefully we'll form a bond no one can tear apart

Those unexpected hugs you give always remind me that you care
Those fun filled times when we watch T.V.
As you ask to comb my hair

It's so important for me to cherish these times
You're growing up so fast
As I watch you mature from a boy to a man
I know the pride I feel will always last

33
A Better Place

Dedicated to Eugene T. Daniels Sr.
R.I.P January 2, 1948-March 20, 2003

A Better Place

I just want to take a little time to express to you how I feel,
I was thinking of you everyday and my love for you is real!
It was hard for me to see you so weak, **this** I can't deny
Why did this have to happen to you?
I wasn't ready for you to die

But when I stop and think, I need to rejoice, because you're no longer suffering or feeling pain
So I thank God for delivering you, because my loss has to be his gain

The memories I want to keep of you are the ones when you were strong and bold
Please continue to watch over me as you walk down those streets of gold

From now on, if I feel like crying, I'll put a smile on my face
Because in my heart I know God's rescued you, and you're in a better place

34
Dear God

Daily inspirational prayer

Dear God

Dear God,

Please continue to walk with me each and everyday
No matter how tough life seems, or how down I might feel, you always make a way

I know that it was nobody but you who has allowed me to tap into this gift I found to write
You have given me an escape route I didn't think was possible
A way to release feelings that for years I've tried to fight

God please don't give up on me, just continue to strengthen me for I want to grow
After all, when my time has expired down here on earth, *heaven* is where I want to go!

35
Loving Yourself

You can't begin to enjoy life if you can't love yourself first!

Loving Yourself

After all this time I think I know exactly what my problem may be
I've searched to find the perfect man, but I never fell in love with me

All this pain, these tears I've cried, feeling depressed and all alone
Lying around, feeling sorry for myself, refusing to answer the phone

What good is this doing, I need to get it together
I need to regain control
As I sit and try to focus on my master plan, I ask the question?
"What's my number one goal?"

So as I looked back on my life, I seemed to realize
No matter who you meet, or how much you have in terms of wealth
None of these things will you be able to enjoy
If you can't first stop, and love yourself!

36
God, My Soul is Tired

Inspired by that feeling you get when you've had all you can take. You request spiritual guidance!

God, My Soul is Tired

I've wanted to be loved for *so* long,
But **never** trusted you!
Placing people in my life that **I** wanted there,
Never praying and seeking proper guidance about what I should do!

I **know** it's not too late
I feel my life has just begun
Just when I felt finding love was a losing battle,
I realized that I have won

No more searching for the right guy whom I feel will make me complete,
I'm turning my heart over to you, so with you, a man would have to compete!

I give up on trying to do this on my own
Now, I am officially retired
I want to be blessed and be loved the right way,
God renew me, for my soul is tired.

Acknowledgements

I would first like to thank God for constantly giving me strength. There were so many times that I felt alone and unmotivated but through God's grace and mercy I was always able to bounce back.

To my biggest fan which is my mother. I love you and thank you for supporting me in everything I do. Thank you for being my personal role model.

I would like to thank my son and daughter for keeping me on my toes. You are a constant reminder that I have so much to live for. I love you and I am determined to help the both of you grow. Andre, you will be a strong black man! Dominique, you will be a respectable young lady!

I would like to thank my brother for always looking out for me. Stay focused and whatever you want to make happen will happen. I love you.

I would like to thank my stepdad for loving my mom so much. Thanks for everything you do for me and my kids. Thank you for treating me like I am one of your own.

I would like to thank my aunt Virginia Payton for keeping me encouraged. Thank you for listening to me and being there when I needed to talk about those things I haven't been so proud of and understanding. I love you from your lil sis!

A special thanks to my father who is no longer with me physically. Emotionally, you are always with me. I love you and want you to be proud of me. I am definitely going somewhere in life.

Thanks to Mrs. Angela Hampton. Girl, you know we've laughed together, cried together, and dreamed together. Thank you for your support and being the kind of friend who accepts that there are always two sides to any story. Even though you have my best interest at heart you always tried to make me think about the situation so I wouldn't make a bad decision. I'll always remember that even those times I wasn't trying to hear it! I love you for being you.

Thanks to Nakea Hughes. The most independent, dependable, and strong. Yet so fragile. I love you! Thank you for being my strength so many times when I was weak and frustrated which is often! Thank you for getting me out the house every time I tried to barricade myself inside after a breakup. Thank you for dealing with and loving me for the person I am.

Thanks to all my friends and family who are cheering me on and know I can do this. I love you too! Like my mom once told me and something I wont forget, "Beware of the Haters."

As crazy as this may sound I want to thank my ex husband for the friendship that only we understand!

Last but not least, I want to thank all the ex boyfriends in my life who have made me a stronger person! There's always one it seems you will never get over no matter how much time goes by. The person who will always hold a special place in your heart. Now I know what it means when people say, "You have to go through to get through."

160

www.ingramcontent.com/pod-product-compliance
Lightning Source LLC
Chambersburg PA
CBHW051758040426
42446CB00007B/421